TO BE OR NOT TO BE

THE ADVENTURE OF CHRISTIAN EXISTENTIALISM

DAVID MOFFETT-MOORE

Energion Publications
Gonzalez, FL
2017

Electronic ISBNs:

iBooks: 978-1-63199-475-3
Kindle: 978-1-63199-476-0
Adobe Digital Editions: 978-1-63199-477-7
Google Play: 978-1-63199-478-4

Print ISBNs:
ISBN10: 1-63199-473-5
ISBN13: 978-1-63199-473-9

Energion Publications
P. O. Box 841
Gonzalez, Florida 32560

pubs@energion.com
energion.com

Acknowledgements

Every thought has many sources and every book has many authors, never just the one who penned it. Existentialism is the search for the meaning of our existence as persons on this planet. I am grateful to every four-year-old that asked the question "Why?" I am grateful to the teachers who taught me to question everything. I am grateful to all who have accompanied me along the pilgrim path that we call life. I am particularly grateful to those who have had a direct influence on this book: Paula Comper and Kyle Tade, colleagues in ministry who previewed the manuscript and caught most of my mistakes; Chris Eyre, my editor in England on whom I can rely to improve upon my product; Bob Cornwall, fellow member of the Academy of Parish Clergy who encouraged me to pursue this endeavor, and especially to Henry Neufeld of Energion Publications, whose encouragement and patience have been amazing.

This is my seventh book, a feat I never dreamed of realizing. In April 2016 I had a stroke while in Ireland. I have lingering side effects that are invisible yet annoying. Henry has been supportive, positive, encouraging and incredibly patient throughout this process.

I am confident there are still mistakes; I am also certain that I have made them!

TO BE OR NOT TO BE:
HAMLET'S QUANDARY

Welcome to the adventure of Christian existentialism. "Adventure" because it is an expression and exploration of the freedom we enjoy to Be, to create meaning in our lives and purpose for our lives. Existentialism is unique among the various schools of philosophy. Where most philosophies seek to be intellectual in their approach and universal in the application, existentialism is intentionally personal, decidedly passionate and unapologetically pragmatic. It is not concerned with why there is life or what is the meaning of life. It is rather concerned with what is the meaning of my life individually and personally. One cannot be entirely objective and detached from one's own existence; existentialism is grounded in the passions. Existentialism further is less concerned about what we think; it is more concerned about how we behave, what we do. In this sense, it is quite pragmatic. Existentialism is intensely personal; therefore our adventure will be through the lives of individuals associated with Existentialism.

The questions and issues of existentialism are played out in William Shakespeare's famous play *Hamlet*, especially expressed in Hamlet's famous soliloquy:

> To be, or not to be: that is the question:
> Whether 'tis nobler in the mind to suffer
> The slings and arrows of outrageous fortune,
> Or to take arms against a sea of troubles,
> And by opposing end them? To die: to sleep;
> No more; and by a sleep to say we end
> The heart-ache and the thousand natural shocks
> That flesh is heir to, 'tis a consummation
> Devoutly to be wish'd.

"What am I going to do with this life of mine?" is the unanswered, and perhaps unanswerable, questions posed by Hamlet's quandary.

To be or not to be? Is there any reason to live at all? Why not just end it all now? Why suffer any discomfort? We are the only creature born knowing that we will die. There was a time before us, and there will be a time after us, and we have little influence, much less control, over either. We stalk and strut about the stage of life but for an instant and then we are gone, and our place knows us no more. What is more, while we are here we are buffeted about by forces we cannot control, forces impervious to and ignorant of our existence. Is life nothing more than a dream, devoid of any meaning or purpose? Are we just the butt of some kind of cruel cosmic joke?

As a tragedy, *Hamlet* is filled with deaths, both intentional and accidental. Hamlet's father dies before the play begins. Polonius is stabbed by Hamlet, thinking him to be Claudius. Grief stricken by Polonius' death, Ophelia drowns herself. Rosencrantz and Guildenstern are killed by the king of England, under orders of Hamlet. Gertrude drinks poison intended for Hamlet. Claudius is stabbed and, just to make sure, poisoned by Hamlet. Laertes is wounded by Hamlet with a poison sword, and Hamlet is poisoned by Laertes. In the end, the only major character left alive is Horatio.

Life is filled with death. Death can be cruel, accidental, unintentional, meaningless. If death is random and meaningless, if we are surrounded by situations and circumstances that are random and meaningless, is not life itself random and meaningless?

Death is the only universal in our human experience. It is as the pilot described flying: the takeoff is optional, the landing is mandatory. Birth may be seen as optional, there being nearly as many miscarriages as there are deliveries. Once born, dying is mandatory. Even Jesus had to die!

If life is meaningless, how can it be noble? How can we be noble? This is the question Hamlet asks: "Whether 'tis nobler in the mind to suffer the slings and arrows of outrageous fortune, or take arms against a sea of troubles, and by opposing, end them?" If life is meaningless, if random influences beyond our control determine much of the course of our lives, if in the end we all lose and die anyway: what are we to do? How are we to live? Can our lives have meaning in a meaningless universe? Can we live a life of cause and purpose when the world denies any cause? In the end this world annihilates us all, how do we live in the face of our own demise?

For some existentialists, suicide is seen as the last act of freedom and self-will. It is certainly an ultimate act. I remember the television show *MASH*, which was staged during the Korean War. In Existentialist fashion, it parodied the futility of human endeavor. The theme song was entitled *Suicide is Painless.* Of course, it is an act that can only be performed once.

Maybe all this talk of death and suicide seems a bit gruesome. Maybe Shakespeare's *Hamlet* seems too stiff. Here is the opening dialog from The Moody Blues' 1969 album *On the Threshold of a Dream.*

First Man: I think, I think I am, therefore I am, I think.

Establishment: Of course you are my bright little star, I've miles and miles of files, pretty files of your forefather's fruit. And now to suit our great computer, you're magnetic ink.

First Man: I'm more than that, I know I am, at least, I think I must be.

Inner Man: There you go man, keep as cool as you can. Face piles and piles of trials with smiles. It riles them to believe that you perceive the web they weave and keep on thinking free.

Existentialism is the adventure of exploring all the possibilities of one's life, experimenting with options and alternatives, and deciding for one's self what the meaning of one's life will be, instead of being a part of some cosmic computer program.

These are the questions we will explore in this search for a Christian Existentialism. We will begin with an introduction to the philosophy of Existentialism, then examine the roots and origins of Existentialism, next explore the branches and fruits of Existentialism, return to a further examination of Secular Existentialism, and finally see if there is any reasonable defense for a response from faith to the Existentialist dilemma. Given the uncertainty of life, how can we live with confidence?

William Ernest Henley suffered from tuberculosis from the age of 12, resulting in having his left leg amputated below the knee. Yet he was determined not to allow his circumstances to determine his character, his surroundings dictate his spirit. He claimed his personhood. This declaration is made clear in his epic poem *Invictus*. It is a poem I memorized as a sophomore in high school. It provided the title for a Nelson Mandela movie starring Morgan Freeman and Matt Damon.

Invictus, by William Ernest Henley

Out of the night that covers me,
Black as the Pit from pole to pole,
I thank whatever gods may be
For my unconquerable soul.

In the fell clutch of circumstance
I have not winced nor cried aloud,
Under the bludgeonings of chance
My head is bloody but unbowed.

Beyond this place of wrath and tears
Looms but the Horror of the shade,
And yet the Menace of the years
Finds, and shall find me unafraid.

It matter not how straight the gate,
How charged with punishments the scroll,
I am the master of my fate;
I am the captain of my soul.

In the face of chaos and confusion, of anxiety and absurdity, of a universe devoid of any great meaning or high purpose, are we yet the masters of our fate and the captains of our soul? We can determine what will be the meaning of our individual lives. Life does not have any inherent meaning; can our lives impart such meaning? We are a meaning-seeking animal, that strange mix of creature and creator whose nature it is to seek meaning and make meaning where there is no meaning. We see patterns where there are no patterns, order where there is only chaos. We look at the night stars and imagine constellations. We gaze at the clouds in the sky and imagine puppies and rabbits. This is how we participate in the divine act of creation: by making meaning.

In Jesus, we see a fellow human who seemed destined to die a most tragic death, yet who chose to commit his life to a nobler meaning, who lived his life in such a way that it stood for something. We are all doomed to die and be forgotten, yet we can choose to live a life of meaning and purpose, of true nobility, in the time that we have. We can make our choice, assert our choice and act on our choice. We can be the master of our fate. This is the essence of Christian Existentialism.

The Existence of Existentialism

Existentialism as a philosophical and literary movement was popularized in the decades after World War II, with roots long before. Where most schools of philosophy are objective, Existentialism is subjective. Where most schools of philosophy are rational, Existentialism emphasizes the passions. Where most schools of philosophy focus on the universal, Existentialism focuses on the individual. Most people we regard as Existentialist would deny and refute that label, claiming that they are too uniquely individual to be grouped with any such school, even one that emphasizes the individual, as Existentialism does.

Existentialism is the individual's pursuit for meaning and purpose in their life. Existentialism is not looking for the meaning of life in a general or universal sense, but in one's individual personal life. It is not the question of Douglas Adams in *The Hitchhikers Guide to the Galaxy*, "What is the meaning of life, the universe and everything?" but rather "What is the meaning and purpose of my life." One can never be totally objective or totally rational about one's own life.

Soren Kierkegaard and Frederick Nietzsche are two philosophers foundational to the Existentialist movement, though neither used the term Existentialism. Kierkegaard lived from 1813 to 1855. Nietzsche lived from 1844 to 1900. Kierkegaard was a Dane; Nietzsche was German. Both grew up in very religious homes with very pious fathers. Both fathers carried a burden of guilt, dread and anxiety. These issues figure strongly in the problems existentialism deals with.

The term Existentialism was first coined by French Catholic philosopher Gabriel Marcel in the 1940s. Many of those we associate with Existentialism did not agree with that association; at first Jean-Paul Sartre rejected the term, but later he confirmed it and published a lecture entitled *Existentialism is a Humanism*.

Sartre and Camus made existentialism important in French thinking, and de Beauvoir extended it to feminist concerns; they built in part on Heidegger's examination of *Being and Time*, while Dostoevsky gave existentialism it's greatest literary expression, while finally Tillich brought existentialism back to Christianity in *The Courage to Be*.

These are the principal names associated with the philosophical school of thought known as Existentialism. There are many other sources influencing its growth and development. There is a strain of existentialism that pervades human history and the history of human thought. There has been much in our society that is influenced by Existentialism, even when they are not comfortable with that label. We next consider the origins of Existentialism.

Roots and Origins

Existentialism began when the first primitive person wondered about their own existence, but we have no record of their questions. So we begin where we do have records, and of course, records of questions.

Heraclitus wrote of the changeability and uncertainty of life, saying "everything changes, nothing remains," and "we can never step twice into the same river." Socrates said "the unexamined life is not worth living." The only life we can truly and fully examine is our own, hence the first Existentialist question. If I want my life to be worth living, I must examine it. The act of examining my life imbues it with meaning. The fact that I examine my life demonstrates that it does indeed have meaning and value, at least to me. Examining life makes it worthy.

Plato was the greatest student of Socrates, it has been said that Plato is philosophy and everything else mere footnotes. Plato's myth of the cave from *The Republic* demonstrates the Existentialist quest. In this myth, we are chained in a cave so that we cannot move. There is a fire behind us giving off light and the wall of the cave before us, where we see shadows dancing. All we know of reality is the shadows. Our knowledge of reality is a far cry from that which is really real. An individual breaks free of their chains, sees that the images on the cave wall are mere shadows of reality and not reality itself. The individual further sees that the fire and the objects casting the shadows are themselves mere fragments of reality. The individual leaves the cave and enters the real world, the true world, the world of trees and animals and flowers. The individual, who has seen ultimate reality and is therefore free, awakened, aware, returns to the cave and tells the others, who are still in chains, what they have seen and what they now know to be real. The individual is presumed to be crazy by the cave dwellers.

This story describes the Existentialist quest and the Existentialist dilemma. The Existentialist wants to find meaning and purpose and worth in their life, but the search for this individualistic meaning seems crazy or foolish or at least misdirected to others. It's very subjectivity makes it suspect. The more free we are as individuals, the more likely we are to be seen by society as crazy. Plato believed that essence precedes existence, that there is an inherent core of being within us, whereas Existentialists believe that existence precedes essence, that we are entirely what we make of ourselves.

Greek mythology gives us several instances of Existentialist thought. Prometheus acts against the gods and brings light and knowledge of fire to humans. He is punished by having vultures consume his liver every day, only to have it grow back at night. He has acted as an individual, expressing his own choice and paying a price for that individual expression. Sisyphus is condemned to roll a giant rock up a hill every day, only to have it roll back down every night. His life is a daily struggle, yet in that struggle he finds his destiny. Icarus flies too high in the heavens, penetrating the realm of the gods, and falls from freedom in the skies to death in the rocks below. Epimetheus is plagued by the forces unleashed by his wife Pandora, yet in his despair and agony is determined to stand by her.

St. Augustine expresses his doubts and questions, his personal struggles, in his *Confessions*. This is not only auto-biographical, it is profoundly psychological, as Augustine shares his inner search for meaning and purpose in his life. This is a personal exposé that is as much psychological as it is spiritual.

Martin Luther's declaration before the Diet in Worms, "Here I stand. God help me, I can do no other." This is an outer expression of his inner struggles and is certainly an example of a person's inner search for meaning and purpose in one's life, a struggle to be true to one's self.

René Descartes's famous dictum "I think, therefore I am." falls within the bounds of the roots of existentialism. The fact that we are a thinking animal, a conscious creature, means that we are aware of our own existence and of our surroundings. It states in a positive form the basic question of existentialism, the question of our existence. It implies that it is our thinking that makes us who and what we are.

Blaise Pascal in the 17th century expresses his concern with the limitations of human existence, the presence of constant change, uncertainty, and suffering in the progress of human life. He introduces the problem of contingency and uncertainty even anti-rationalism in individual existence. These are all issues that later Existentialist philosophers will also wrestle with.

Immanuel Kant describes the limits of human reason and even human experience, and in these limitations, introducing themes common to the Existentialists. We can't directly experience the outer world. We can only directly experience the inner world. We experience the outer world through the instrument and filter of our senses. However, unlike Kant, the existentialists do not believe there is any categorical imperative, any universal objective truth. The Scottish philosopher David Hume, in his psychological basis of human nature and his belief that the passions, not reason govern behavior, is also a precursor of existentialism. He claimed reason to be a slave of the passions and that all knowledge must come from our experience. He said that even our sense of ethics and morality is based upon sentiment and emotion.

Human history is replete with examples of Existentialism. To be human is to ask the question why am I here, what is the meaning and purpose of my life, what is my calling and my destiny. The quest for meaning in one's own life is necessarily personal, subjective, passionate, emotional. It is a quest that defines us. It is a quest that we cannot help but embark on. We must do this, by our very nature. To be human is to ask why.

THE EXISTENTIALIST QUEST

Now we explore some of the issues related to Existentialism. Existentialism holds that existence precedes essence. That is to say, we have no thought prior to experience. The most important concern for us as individuals is that we are individuals, acting independently of one another and each responsible for our own choices and actions. Most of the time we do not know what the consequences of our choices and actions will be, but we are responsible for those consequences nonetheless. In the midst of uncertainty we must decide. We cannot know the consequences of those decisions, yet we are accountable for those consequences. This is part of the Existentialist dilemma. We are subjective thinkers. The single most important fact about our existence is our own consciousness, even though that consciousness may be nothing more than the accumulated affect of our experiences.

A second issue for existentialism is absurdity. I am my own existence, but this existence is absurd. We live in a world that has no inherent meaning. The universe is entirely indifferent to our existence. There is no meaning in the world beyond the meaning that we ascribe to the world. Anything can happen at any time to anyone. This means that it's not "why do bad things happen to good people" but rather "things happen to people." Good and bad are indifferent, even irrelevant terms. The Existentialist would say "stuff happens, deal with it!" There are no absolutes. As Gertrude Stein wrote, "There ain't no answer. There ain't going to be any answer. There never has been an answer. That's the answer."

Living in this absurd universe fills us with anxiety, which is a third issue for Existentialists we live in a daily sense of dread, a generalized uneasiness, and atmosphere of anxiety. Anxiety is a universal condition of human existence. When we realize that we live in a meaningless universe, where we are limited to a partial understanding of even our own experiences, and yet we must make decisions on how to live, we can't help but be anxious. In other words, if you're not at least a little bit anxious, you don't understand the situation!

Even though I live in a meaningless universe, I want my life to have meaning. Even though I live in the midst of absurdity and am filled with anxiety, I seek authenticity. This striving for authenticity, to be a genuine self, a true individual, is another issue for Existentialism. Humans are social creatures. Our evolutionary existence depends upon our ability to cooperate with one another. We form communities and civilizations. We are born into families, and we live in neighborhoods. We are innately members of a group. The challenge is for us to find ourselves and be true to ourselves, rather than lose ourselves and lose our individuality to herd mentality.

Alienation is another issue for existentialism. As I grow in my understanding of myself as an individual, and affirm myself as an individual, I am necessarily alienated from my environment. As I am myself, I am alienated from the other. I am alienated from other people in my environment, and I am alienated from that environment itself. The more aware I am of myself, the more aware I am of the otherness of the other. Part of our dilemma is that we must either be alienated from others or alienated from ourselves; it is inevitable that we are alienated from something. Our consciousness as creatures sensing our experiences and seeking understanding leads inevitably to alienation.

Our final issue for existentialism is the existence of the unknown, the nothingness, the void. We dance our lives suspended above the abyss. This is what William Ernest Henley, in his poem "Invictus," describes as the night that is black as the pit. We cannot be certain of anything. We cannot even know all that we do not know. Our understanding is in part, our knowledge based on uncertainties. The ultimate unknown is death, when we cease to exist. It is what Hamlet describes as that dread, "the undiscovered country, from whose bourn no traveler returns." For the existentialist, death might be seen as the final freedom.

Existentialism asserts that existence precedes essence, before we can understand we must experience and before we can experience we must exist, and the reality of our existence is our primal and lifelong problem. We live in an absurd universe and our lives are themselves an absurdity, and this fills us with anxiety. In this existence where the outer world is absurd and the inner world is anxious, we yet strive to be authentic human beings, authentic individuals. This drive for authenticity results in our alienation from all that surrounds us. Beyond this world that we have experienced and may have some understanding of remains only the void, the vast unknown of which death itself is the only final solution. Welcome to existentialism!

THE BRANCHES AND FRUITS OF EXISTENTIALISM

Just as the roots and sources of existentialism run deep throughout human history, so the branches and fruits of existentialism can be found throughout all forms of human self-expression existentialism is a not bound by the limits of philosophy; it can be found throughout the arts and letters. Sartre, Camus and Dostoyevsky have already been mentioned; there are many others. Other authors range from Franz Kafka, Herman Hesse and Kurt Vonnegut and Jack Kerouac and Philip K Dick.

In Hamlet, quoted earlier, the lead character must deal with the certainty of death and the uncertainty of life. He anguishes over his decisions. The play is filled with plot twists, depicting the unexpected uncertainties of life.

Dostoyevsky's novels are filled with a richness of existentialist dilemmas. In *The Brothers Karamozov*, the grand inquisitor protects the people from the risks of freedom that Jesus offers. In *Crime and Punishment*, our protagonist is riddled with guilt that proves to be his undoing. *In Notes from the Underground*, he argues that humans are not rational but emotional creatures which proves to be the undoing of society.

Cinema likewise runs the gamut. In *The Matrix* one must choose between the red pill or the blue pill, between a pleasant dream or a painful reality, where waking up is the nightmare and we must see through the illusions to the truth hidden behind. In *Fight Club* we are engaged in the struggle of life, self-awareness and becoming a true individual. In *Apocalypse Now* Col. Kurtz, played by Marlon Brando, rises above the crowd to create himself as a new and free individual, yet he is insane, the setting is absurd. In *Groundhog Day* we are trapped in an endless loop, doomed to repeat the same trivial, meaningless day over and over. All these have expression to issues and problems of existentialism. What could be more existentialist than *Monty Python's the Meaning of Life*? If life has a meaning, it is trivial. Read a book, take a walk, be nice.

Theater has also been a home to existentialist questions. In John Paul Sartre's *No Exit*, we find that hell is other people. In Tom Stoppard's *Rosencrantz and Guildenstern are Dead*, two throw away characters from Hamlet become central figures debating the meaning of their existence, yet in *Hamlet* their importance is only that they die. In Samuel Beckett's *Waiting for Godot*, the character Godot never arrives and all we do is wait. They all give expression to questions and concerns of existentialism. The very name of the genre, theater of the absurd, declares itself to be part and parcel of the existentialist pursuit. M. C. Escher's famous lithographs depict our human effort to find order out of chaos and make sense of the absurd is a depict images that could never exist in reality.

Psychology has also been greatly influenced the questions and struggles of existentialism. Rollo May helps us reconnect our individuality with existence. Carl Rogers inspires us to be fully functional individuals. Victor Frankl writes of our human need for meaning and the power that finding or forming such meaning can have in our lives. He says what matters is not the meaning of life in general but the immediate meaning of an individual's life at a particular moment. Ernest Becker confronts us with our fear of freedom in our denial of death. In the first phase of our life, Sigmund Freud writes of our pursuit of passion. In the middle phase of our life, Adler writes of our pursuit of power. The final phase of our life, Carl Jung writes of our pursuit of purpose.

In all these human activities and pursuits, and all these many and varied ways we have for self-expression, we see continued the questions, the problems, issues of existentialism. It is a part of who we are. To be human is to experience our existence. To experience existence is to question that existence. Through the discipline of philosophy, through the study of psychology, through theater and movies and novels, we express the questions and the conditions of our existence, the joys and celebrations, the fears and the anxieties. Again, to be human is to ask the question, "Why?"

The Existentialists: Who Are They?

One must be careful in classifying people as existentialists. One of the principal characteristics of existentialism is individuality; many who may be regarded as existentialists rejected that label for themselves. Still, there are a number of philosophers who are widely called existentialists even over their objections.

Soren Kierkegaard

Soren Kierkegaard must be regarded as the seminal existentialist philosopher. He was born May 5, 1813 in Copenhagen, Denmark and died November 11, 1855 in Copenhagen. He lived all his life in and around the city of Copenhagen. He never used

13

the term Existentialist to describe himself, preferring instead to describe his life journey as a quest to become an individual. While outwardly his life may appear to be uneventful, his inner life is filled with the struggle of anxiety. Kierkegaard's father was a prosperous and pious businessman, yet also filled with guilt and gloom. He was haunted by the memory of having cursed God as a boy, and having impregnated his wife before they were married shortly after the death of his first wife. He believed that all his children would die before the age of 34, the traditional age at which Christ died on the cross. Kierkegaard's father died when he was only 25, but the relationship lingered throughout his life. The younger Kierkegaard doubtless absorbed some of his father's sense of guilt and dread. While a student at the University, Kierkegaard was introduced to the philosophy of Hegel, which influenced him in a negative way. Kierkegaard rebelled against Hegel's world spirit, which downplayed the influence and role of the individual. Kierkegaard would strongly criticize Hegel's viewpoint.

Kierkegaard met Regina Olson when she was only 15 years old. After a long courtship and became engaged in 1840, however, less than a year later, he broke off the engagement claiming he could not make her happy. He would later regret this decision and seek to reinstate the engagement. She declined and married another. Kierkegaard would never marry, and would later write that he regarded engagement as binding as marriage itself. In his will, he left his entire estate to Regina, who declined it.

Kierkegaard was a prolific writer, and often wrote under various pseudonyms. In addition to philosophy, he wrote novels, essays and reviews. Late in his life engaged in a battle of wits of sorts with the magazine entitled the Corsair. They engaged in satirical criticism of one another and Kierkegaard took it to heart. Evidently he could give it better than he could take it. This was a cause of depression that he carried with him.

Kierkegaard also spent his life arguing against the Church of Denmark. He found institutionalized religion and the established church to be the antithesis of true religion and authentic individuality. He found that organized religion was too lenient and let people off too easily. For himself, Kierkegaard always struggled for an authentic faith experience and had a sense of dread the divine. He said it was necessary to introduce Christianity into Christendom.

Kierkegaard experienced worship in the established church as a congregation passively watching while the pastor and choir participated in worship. He said that instead, pastor and choir rightly serve as stagehands while the congregation is actively engaged in worship and God is the appreciative audience, enjoying the play of God's children. Although he spent his career defending and rescuing an authentic Christianity, even in his last year he confessed "I dare not call myself a Christian."

FRIEDRICH NIETZSCHE

In some sense, we go one extreme to another moving from Kierkegaard to Nietzsche. The two held many opposing views. Yet they also share some commonality in their upbringing and influences. Nietzsche was born October 15, 1854 near Leipzig. His father was a very strict Lutheran minister who died when Frederick was only five years old he grew up in a household of women: his mother, grandmother, two aunts, and younger sister. It was a strict household that had the cloak of Christianity but not the compassion. Like Kierkegaard, Nietzsche would criticize traditional reality and religion and traditional values. He would, of course, come up with his own alternatives and conclusions. Intellectually brilliant, Nietzsche would earn two doctorates and gained a university chair at the age of 24, a truly rare accomplishment. He was also a prolific writer. His writings influence wider German intellectual culture, and he was for a time family friend of Richard Wagner.

Later in his life, his health failed him forced to resign as university position, although he did continue writing he suffered from headaches, nausea, eye trouble, possibly had a brain tumor, suffered from bouts of dementia, contracted syphilis. He wintered in Italy and summered in Switzerland. He collapsed in the street in Turin. He died of a stroke, complicated by pneumonia in 1900. His younger sister Elizabeth, in charge of his legacy, compiled and edited his unpublished writings, but too frequently interjected her own sentiments. During his lifetime, Nietzsche was not a nation-

15

alist and did not consider himself to be a German. His sister had strong anti-Semitic opinions and would interject her thoughts to his. This has led to some misconceptions and false judgments about Nietzsche and his philosophy.

Nietzsche believed that life comes to us meaningless and it is our task to create value, meaning and even ourselves. He decried what he called slave morality, going along with the crowd, fitting in and getting by, living an anonymous life. He praises instead the Overman, sometimes called the Superman, the one who claims and lives his or her own life and making their own way. Becoming an individual and being the noble, claiming our power. Nietzsche would decry the masses who live their anonymous lives slave morality of getting by and getting along. Nietzsche would challenge us to claim our lives and we live our lives, rejecting the dogmas of the past and finding our own way. Life is about power and the claim to power one's life Nietzsche would understand Christianity as a slave morality. He proclaims that God is dead and we have killed God. The substance and structure of our society is lost all its meaning, and we are compelled to find a new way with no resources other than ourselves.

NIETZSCHE'S NOBILITY

Nietzsche contrasts the goal of nobility with the slave mentality. The Noble is the person who is in control of themselves who accepts and approves of themselves, who is in charge of their life. Like Heraclitus, the Noble embrace change. The Noble strives to be an individual. This requires personal power; the Noble see themselves as being powerful and being vital, being truly alive and fully free. By contrast Slave mentality is to blend in rather than stand out. Slave mentality rejects individuality and seeks to be part of the crowd, part of the herd. Where the Noble is full of life, the slave is full of fear.

Is God Dead?

Nietzsche is famous for his declaration "God is dead." God is dead and we have killed him. What does he mean by this? What kind of God is it that can be dead?

I think the understanding of God as being a being, a creature, is passé. As Tillich said, God is not a being but God is being-ness itself. God is the ground of all being. Even Aquinas asserted that God is not a being among other beings. The idea of God being some big guy in the sky is no longer meaningful. The idea of God as being a universal ultimate meaning for all people is dead. God does not have a plan for my life that I must discover and obediently follow; there is no predestination. It is my responsibility to find my own meaning for my life. The idea of a personal deity available at my beck and call is dead. By calling these descriptions of God as being dead, I mean they are no longer meaningful and no longer adequate.

If we understand God as that which causes to be, then as long as there is existence, creation, there must be that which causes existence and creation. Paul Tillich's description of God as the ground of all being is more appropriate. In saying God is dead, we mean there are no absolutes, no universal meaning. We mean that life does not have any universal inherent meaning. It is up to us to make sense out of our own existence. We are responsible for our own being.

I have a beautiful little book entitled *Schott's Original Miscellany* that has two pages of philosophical quotations. The first is from Frederick Nietzsche, "God is dead: but considering the state the species of man is in, there will perhaps be caves, for ages yet, in which his shadow will be shown." The last quote is from Leo Tolstoy, the great Russian novelist and devout Christian, "Frederick Nietzsche was stupid and abnormal." Of course, both statements may be true. Given that Nietzsche went insane and died with syphilis, Tolstoy may not be far off.

The idea of there being a divine being somewhere up there that personally and intimately participates in our lives is dead. I am more likely to believe in a God that is like the Force in *Star Wars*. Permeating all creation, beneath and before and behind and above, within all living things, influencing the flow of history and the course of evolution on a grand scale. Tillich's "That which causes to be." Quantum physics speculates on an m-field, an energy field permeates the universe and that holds all things together; this might be a more apt analogy in the 21st century for the divine.

Certainly the God of antiquity is dead. The God of the ancients is dead. The God as a tribal overlord or storm God or one that sits in the clouds throwing thunderbolts upon the earth is dead. The God that is not a person or a being, but that is being-ness itself rather than a being, that is less a creature and more creation itself, may yet be very much alive.

Martin Heidegger

Martin Heidegger born September 26, 1889 in Messkirch, Germany. He enjoyed a quiet, conservative, religious upbringing, even spending a very brief time with the Jesuits before leaving to study theology. Studied under Husserl and served as an assistant, eventually filling Husserl's chair on his retirement. He dedicated his magnum opus, *Being and Time*, to Husserl, *Being and Time* established Heidegger in the intellectual community of Europe. Heidegger's philosophical awakening was in his encounter with Aristotle's *Metaphysics*. Aristotle's understanding of being and being-ness or is-ness drives Heidegger's philosophy. Heidegger's concept of Dasein referred to our being self-aware, our being-in-the-world, grounded and whole. He described the arbitrariness of existence as being thrown into the world. In 1933 Heidegger joined the Nazi party and worked to bring university education in line with Hitler's political program. He left the University in 1934 but did not leave the party, and he never fully and clearly repudiated his association with the Nazis. After the war he was temporarily banned from teaching. He continued to work with problem of existence and the concept of being throughout his career. Heidegger died on May 26, 1976.

THE FRENCH CONNECTION

We have looked at our Teutonic trio of existentialists in Kierkegaard, Nietzsche and Heidegger. Now it is time to turn our attention to the French connection of Sartre, Camus and de Beauvoir.

JEAN-PAUL SARTRE

Jean-Paul Sartre was born in Paris June 21, 1905 and died in Paris April 15, 1980. His father was an officer in the Navy and died while overseas when Sartre was only two years old His mother was a first cousin of Albert Schweitzer. She remarried when Sartre was 12 years old they moved and he was frequently bullied while growing up. He was in frail health and only grew to a height of 5 feet so he was an easy target. He was a noted prankster and satirist. He was drafted into the French Army in 1929 and served to 1931. His experience at this time convinced him that all French were responsible for the atrocities of the war for independence in Algeria. He was drafted again in 1939 captured and served as a prisoner of war. During this time he read Heidegger's *Being and Time*, which proved a great influence on his thinking. In 1929 he met the equally intellectual Simone de Beauvoir, with whom he had a lifelong non-monogamous relationship.

After World War II Sartre remained quite active politically. He was pro-communist, pro-Marxist and a political agitator, arrested for civil disobedience just a few years before his death. He went to Cuba, met Castro, and proclaimed Che Guevara the most perfect man, whose thoughts best matched his actions. Sartre was a chain smoker and a heavy user of amphetamines, which caused his health to deteriorate. He became nearly blind. In 1964 he was awarded the Nobel Prize in literature, which he refused to accept. When he died, over 50,000 attended his funeral. He was well loved and respected by the French.

Of all the Existentialists, Sartre was probably the most comfortable with the title he wrote an essay in its defense entitled "Existentialism is a Humanism". In this essay he argues that existence precedes essence, that is to say, we are born without any essential meaning or purpose in our lives. First we exist. In that existence we establish our own essence is a great masterpiece, *Being and Nothingness*, was published in 1943. It is his response to Heidegger's *Being and Time*. Sartre would say that we are doomed to be free, we must deliver lives and make our choices. We choose how to understand our situation how to relate in our situation and how to respond to our situation our choices are our own. Life is less what happens to us than it is what we choose to do with what happens to us. We always have choices, however uncomfortable some of them might be. Being human means to be free, to be free means to be responsible. We must choose, and we are responsible for our choices. Our choices and our actions create the value and meaning and purpose in our lives. In his political action and civil disobedience, Sartre lived out his choices late into his life.

ALBERT CAMUS

Albert Camus was born November 7, 1913 in French Algeria his mother was Spanish and deaf in one ear; his father was an agricultural worker wounded during World War I and died of those wounds. His mother was an illiterate housecleaner, and they lived without many possessions or comforts throughout Camus's childhood. He enjoyed playing soccer but he contracted tuberculosis in 1930 and had to give up his athletic activities. He continued to struggle financially, balancing studies with part-time jobs for income in 1935 he joined the Communist Party as a way to fight inequalities between Europeans and Algerians.

Camus did not consider himself to be an Existentialist even though he was often called one he confessed that both he and Sartre were surprised to see their names linked. He also said he did not believe in God though he also said he was not an atheist. Camus considered marriage to be unnatural and claimed not to be cut out for marriage. He had frequent affairs along with his serial marriages. He was an author, novelist, and journalist, being awarded the Nobel Prize in literature. He was active politically, against the French in Algeria, against the Germans in France during World War II, and as a communist and an anarchist. He died in a car accident at the age of 46. Camus may be regarded as the conscience of existentialism.

He was quite compassionate as well is passionate, and he rebelled against what he saw as life's injustices. Death itself is an injustice and it makes our lives and absurdity, yet it is the inevitability of our death that invigorates our life. Life may be absurd, but we can live it with authenticity.

SIMONE DE BEAUVOIR

Simone de Beauvoir was born January 9, 1908 in Paris and died April 14 in 1986 also in Paris. She is the only woman in this mix of existentialist philosophers. Her father was a frustrated actor her mother from the upper class; her family struggled to maintain its status. Simone was sent to prestigious private schools. In her childhood she was a deeply religious girl and anticipated becoming a nun. At the age of 14 she faced a crisis of faith and the rest of her life she was a self-proclaimed atheist. She was intellectually brilliant and the equal of anyone on this list. Her father would boast that she thought like a man. I doubt she saw that as a true compliment. She met John Paul Sartre as they were studying together and they began a lifelong relationship. They never married, Simone saying she couldn't because she had no dowry. Neither were they monogamous; Simone had a number of lesbian relationships including several with her students.

Simone's great work was entitled *The Second Sex*, a passionate and intellectual argument for the abolition of sexism and the myth of the eternal feminine. She argues that women are fully equal to and independent of men. Men have treated women as "the other". They are independent human beings in their own selves and do not need a man to be considered whole. She might agree with Gloria Steinem's quote "A woman without a man is like a fish without a bicycle." Her life is an example of Existentialism lived out: she made her choices independently of others and society in general, and individually.

FYODOR DOSTOEVSKY

Fyodor Dostoyevsky was born November 11, 1821 and died February 9, 1881. He was a Russian novelist author essayist journalist and philosopher. He was raised in a very religious family, learning the Bible at an early age. He attended services regularly, religious instruction and annual pilgrimages. As an adult he would recite his childhood prayers and passages from the book of Job that impressed him while he was a child. His mother died when he was 15 years of age. He described himself as a child of unbelief and doubt, and at the same time choosing to be with Christ rather than with truths if forced to choose.

He graduated from a military Institute and worked as an engineer while writing his first novel, enjoying a lavish lifestyle and social life. He was arrested for belonging to the wrong a kind of literary group sentenced to death at the last minute commuted. He spent four years in a Siberian prison camp followed by six years of compulsory military service in exile. Following this he returned to writing and traveling through Western Europe. Dostoyevsky was influenced by wide variety of philosophers and likewise influenced many other authors and philosophers. His novels deal with religious psychological and political issues of the day. In his novels, Dostoyevsky's protagonists struggle with the issues popular among existentialists. They appreciate the use of literature in philosophy because it speaks to the emotions is not dogmatic it is concrete vivid, and it allows them to deal with the issues of their philosophy.

FRANZ KAFKA

Franz Kafka was born July 3, 1883 and died June 3, 1924. He was part of a middle-class German-speaking Jewish family in Prague, part of the Czech Republic today, but at that time part of the Austro-Hungarian Empire. He was trained as a lawyer employed by an insurance company, which meant his writing was in his spare time. He was engaged to several women who he never married. He died at the age of 40 from tuberculosis. Few of his works were published during his lifetime. After his death he was hailed as the Dante of the 20th century and ranked among the greatest writers of our time. He wrote of isolated protagonists facing bizarre predicaments and incomprehensible bureaucratic powers, His themes include alienation and persecution, struggle and solitude. His protagonists struggle against absurdities they face in an effort to find their authenticity, to become true individuals. They try to make sense of the absurd. His writings are quite popular with existentialists, as they deal in literary forms with the issues of existentialism.

The novel *The Trial* is an excellent example. In it, the protagonist is arrested and put on trial, without ever being told what he is accused of he is a man condemned to make sense of what does not make sense. He is alone against the machine. He hires a lawyer that is of no use, he encounters a priest who of no benefit, he confronts a doorkeeper who refuses to let him use the door that has been expressly prepared for him. His innocence is irrelevant, the truth is irrelevant, all that matters is the machine. Life is absurd and we cannot understand it, we can only struggle against it. In the end, we die. It is absurd, yet it is all we have.

COMING TO AMERICA

Finally we come to America, in the form of Paul Tillich. Paul Tillich was born August 20, 1886 in a small village in the province of Brandenburg in Germany. He was the oldest of three, with two sisters, one of whom died young. His Prussian father was a conservative Lutheran pastor. As a boy, Tillich was sent to boarding schools where he experienced much loneliness. When he was 17, his mother died of cancer. After attending several universities, Tillich received his philosophy and theology degrees and became an ordained Lutheran minister himself. He joined the Imperial German Army as chaplain. His first wife left him for another, and Tillich did remarry. When Hitler came to power, Tillich was dismissed from his teaching position. Reinhold Niebuhr visited Germany from America and convinced Tillich to accept a position at Union theological seminary in New York City. At the age of 47, Tillich came to America. From 1933 until 1955, he taught at Union theological seminary in a variety of positions. 1955 to 1962 he taught at Harvard University. 1962 to his death in 1965, he taught at the University of Chicago.

While Tillich established his reputation in academic circles based on his massive three volumes of *Systematic Theology*, he may more easily be approached in his brief or and more popular books.

Their titles reveal their connection to existentialism. *Shaking the Foundations, The Dynamics of Faith, The Courage to Be, The New Being.* Tillich is regarded as one of the most influential theologians of the 20th century it was quite popular as a teacher and preacher. At Harvard he was the only faculty member who would attend Billy Graham's revivals. His shorter works are quite popular with the general public. He wrote of the struggle between being and non-being and described God not as a being but rather as the ground of all being, as being-ness itself. He described faith as our ultimate concern and God as a matter of ultimate concern. Whatever is our ultimate concern, that is our god. Courage is our response to anxiety, our anxiety in facing death, our anxiety in facing our natural guilt, and our anxiety in facing our aimlessness. With courage, we proclaim our being.

KIERKEGAARD'S STAGES OF LIFE

Kierkegaard describes three stages in life development: the aesthetic, the ethical and the religious. The first two stages are inauthentic and unsatisfactory. Only the third stage is authentic and free. The aesthetic avoids commitments and seeks pleasurable experiences, immediate personal gratification without regard for consequences. The aesthete stage includes three different states. There is the unconscious state, who goes through life avoiding thought and avoiding feeling. There is the hedonistic state that seeks the pleasure principle. And there is the reflective state, day-dreaming through life reflecting on possibilities to the exclusion of reality. The ethical person finds their place in life and fills out that role. They subordinate themselves to the will of society. They make good "company man". The ethical person can hide behind rules and regulations.

The religious person is authentic and free. The religious person has taken what Kierkegaard calls "the leap of faith." They are willing to give up what they have and what they have become for the sake of what they may yet they have grown beyond the pleasures of the present moment and the roles and rules of society.

Kierkegaard was at war with the institution of Christendom. The Church in his time was a national church. If you are a Dane you are a member. The Church was essentially an extension of the state and of the society. This is not what Kierkegaard meant by religion or by faith. Faith means to be bold, to be passionate, to be lively to be vigorous. Kierkegaard would say the members of the Church of Denmark did not have faith, rather they lacked faith. Faith is not a habit or custom, it is a daringness, a stretching out, and openness, indeed, a leap. Faith is daring be one's own true, real, free self. Kierkegaard's faith is what GK Chesterton spoke of when he said "Christianity has not been tried and found wanting, it has been found difficult and left untried." For Kierkegaard, the religious life is a rich life, a full life, a life bold enough to set sail on the uncertain see of this indeterminate world.

MANY PATHS, ONE MOUNTAIN

The question of personal meaning is one that has occupied humanity as long as we have had self-awareness. We have been looking particularly at the Existentialist, but the search for personal meaning is part of the modern quest for identity and one with which many have wrestled.

It could be said that the psychology of Sigmund Freud is most relevant for us as young adults, when we are most strongly influenced by our hormones. Our sexuality is a strong part of our sense of self. The writings of Alfred Adler on the quest for power may be most appropriate for our middle years, when we are striving to pursue our careers and establish our families. Carl Jung says that every issue past midlife is essentially a spiritual issue, a question of meaning. So we can benefit by applying Freud to our younger years, Adler to our middle years, and Jung to our later years.

Jung sees the quest for individuation, as he calls it, to be a lifelong journey for us. In his hierarchy of needs, Alfred Adler calls it "individual psychology." Abraham Maslow describes self-actualization as a supreme personal accomplishment. Murray Bowen, in his family systems theory, describes the process of self-differentiation. Victor Frankl's logotherapy is the tool used in his existential analysis for *Man's Search for Meaning*. All of this certainly is what Kierkegaard described as a true individual.

James Fowler describes different stages of faith formation as part of human development. The primal, incorporative self from birth to 2; the intuitive protective, impulsive self from 2-6; the mythic, literal, imperial self from 7 – 11+; the synthetic-conventional faith of the interpersonal self of adolescence; the exclusive, individuative-reflective faith of the institutional self that some of us never outgrow. The last two stages develop as we become critically self-aware; the conjunctive faith of the inter-individuative self, that recognizes polarities and paradox and myth and metaphor; and the inclusive universalizing faith of the God-grounded self, that manifests openness to the power of being and a passionate detachment. These final two stages of Fowler's might align with Kierkegaard's Religious stage, Maslow's self-actualized and Bowen's self-differentiated.

Each of these thinkers in their own way pursues a common interest, though each by a different name and along a different path. What does it mean to be a complete human being, a mature person, a whole self, to be fulfilled? Whether we call it individuation, self-actualization, differentiation, existential analysis, or the individual, we are describing several paths climbing the same mountain. It is the mountain of self discovery and self creation in determining and declaring who we are as individual human beings in our own selves.

A Christian Existentialism

How can there be a Christian existentialism? Existentialism tells us life has no inherent meaning. Existentialism declares that God is dead. Existentialism has led some to nihilism. Existentialism says if there is no inherent value then there can be no inherent ethics or morals. Many of its early proponents were atheists. Many of them lived lives that were not models of traditional Christian behavior. Given all this, how can there be a Christian existentialism?

There is a much in Existentialism that we find attractive, even compelling. The three themes that run throughout Existentialism are its emphasis on the individual, the role of the passions, and the importance of freedom. All of these are very life affirming. Most schools of philosophy look at humanity in general; existentialism uniquely lifts up the importance of the individual and of being an individual. Most schools of philosophy emphasize the role of reason over emotion; Existentialism challenges us to live passionate lives.

Some schools of philosophy counsel us to find our place and fill it, to pursue our destiny, our calling; Existentialism offers us the freedom of finding our own way and blazing our own path. Existentialism urges us to live our lives to the fullest, knowing that what that looks like will be different for each individual. We are to be our own unique selves. Some of the founders of Existentialism have been atheists, some have not. Kierkegaard was determined to be Christian. Dostoyevsky likewise was devout in his faith. Paul Tillich taught and wrote a new form of Christian theology. There is nothing inherent in Existentialism that prevents it being a philosophy that allows for, encourages, and makes sense of faith.

Christian existentialism places supreme value on the role of the individual. We are responsible for our choices and our actions. How we behave is more important than what we believe. We act out our faith. Psychoanalysis suggests that examining our behavior will reveal what we truly, even subconsciously believe, as an operational definition of our faith. The epistle of James challenges us, suggesting that if we say we have faith we must demonstrate it in our deeds; in his deeds, James says, he will prove his faith. Existentialism consistently emphasizes the role of action over attitudes, of behavior over belief, of practice over principle. What we do and how we live testifies to who we are. Likewise, Christian Existentialism says that we each stand or fall on our own merits. Paul writes in Romans 2:6, that each one of us will be judged according to our deeds; this is repeated in 1 Corinthians 5:10, we must each appear on our own, according to what we have done, good or bad. There is certainly a call to the community of faith, to the fellowship of believers, but this does not take precedence over our responsibility as individuals. How many times have we said that if only one life needed saving, Christ would still have come. Each person is of infinite value and worth, each life is worth living. We spend our lives in an effort to be who we are, to be true to ourselves as we understand ourselves to be. We do this as individuals. It is as Kierkegaard himself testified, a lifelong struggle to be an individual and to be a Christian, understanding the two to be but one.

In John 21 the risen Christ visits with the disciples. He asked Peter three times if Peter loved him, which Peter affirmed. Christ warns Peter that he will be led where he does not want to go. Peter asks what about John, what will happen to John? Jesus says that is none of Peter's business. In this scene, Jesus relates to and deals with each disciple separately and in turn. He deals with them and relates with them as individuals. In 1 Corinthians, Paul warns the church about divisions within the church. He asks who is Peter, who is Apollos, who is Paul? One plants, one waters, one tends. Each has their purpose, their role. They each serve in their turn, as individuals. Peter is not Apollos, Apollos is not Paul. They each best serve the common good by being true to themselves as unique individuals.

Christian Existentialism challenges us to be our best and truest self, to be who we are as individuals. The creation account in Genesis says that we are formed in the image and likeness of God. God is the ultimate creator; the image and likeness of God, then, must be that of creator. I've long believed that we are created incomplete as individuals, in the hope that we will participate in God's creation by completing and finishing our own creation. This includes our not having an inherent or essential meaning or purpose. As creative creatures in the Creator's creation, we are to create even our own meaning and purpose. That is a part of our own act of creation.

Christian Existentialism also places priority on the passions over reason and rationality, reversing the position of most schools of philosophy. This is evident in the supreme act of the Christian gospel, which is the crucifixion and resurrection of Jesus. We call this moment of singularity, "the passion of Christ." The Gospels are filled with occasions when Jesus is deeply powerfully moved. The King James version describes Jesus as moved in his bowels. The Greek might more accurately be translated Jesus moved in his womb. More modern translations describe Jesus as moved with compassion. What is compassion but moved with passion? Jesus is described as a man of emotion. He is angry enough to lead a riot in the temple. He weeps at the death of his friend Lazarus. He confronts demons and disciples alike. I like to think of Christianity as a reasonable faith, a faith that makes sense; but no one ever became Christian because it was logical. Kierkegaard's leap of faith is not logical, it is passionate and emotional.

In the book of Job, Job is tested and tried to prove the genuineness of his faith. He complains of all the hardship he endures, all the challenges he encounters. He is advised simply to curse God and die, and he defiantly responds, "even though God slay me, yet will I love God!" This is a declaration of passion. I am reminded of Dostoyevsky's confession that if he ever had to choose between Christ and the truth, he would choose to stay with Christ. A declaration of loyalty that is an act of will and emotionally charged, not based on reason or logic. I am not a Christian because it makes sense; I am a Christian because I have been so deeply loved.

Christian existentialism places equal priority on our human freedom. As creatures who are created to finish their own creation, we must be formed free. There is not a cookie-cutter out there somewhere that we are supposed to end up looking like. We are formed to be fully free. As Paul says in Galatians, it is for our freedom that Christ has set us free. In Romans 7, when Paul complains and confesses that he cannot do the good he would do, but instead does the wrong he would not do, he also declares that Christ has set us free from the limitations of our own mortality the finiteness of our creatureliness. In 1 Corinthians 15, where Paul confronts the reality of our deaths, he again declares the sting of death and the power of the grave have been overcome by the victory of Christ. So Christian existentialism sets us free from our finiteness, from our limitations, even from our own deaths. We are born free, formed free, live free and even die free. So great is the importance of our human freedom in Christian existentialism.

I believe that free will means we are free creatures living in a free universe. The future is not pre-packaged and waiting for us to open. The future is ours to create. Even God waits to see what we will make of ourselves and of the creation that we participate in. My steps are not laid out for me, God has no path waiting for me to discover it. My life is my own, to make of it as I will. As Christians, we believe that God is love and that God loves us, each one, unconditionally. Love requires freedom. Love seeks to give itself in love to the object of that love and desires to receive love in return. Love cannot be forced. In spite of the song, I cannot make anyone love me. Love must be free. If God is love, then we must have free will. We must be free creatures living in a free universe. We are free even in that creation.

The focus on the individual, centrality of the passions and emotion, and the importance of human freedom and free will are the three fundamental priorities in existentialism and in Christian existentialism. They are consistent with the Christian faith and the testimony of scripture. They are not the only way, but they are certainly an acceptable and appropriate way to be Christian. I am reminded again of the line from GK Chesterton, "the way of Christianity has not been tried and found wanting; it has been found difficult and left untried." Any form of existentialism is not for the weak and timid, but for the brave and the daring. In terms of individuality, Christian existentialism says I am the only me that is going to be. There is no pattern to trace nor path to follow. There is no plan B. I am the only me this universe will ever see. The challenge is for me to be my own best and truest self, to be authentic, to be an individual. This challenge will require all I have to give, my heart and soul and mind and strength, my reason and my emotion. It is not a logical act, but a passionate one. The passion of the Christian is no less than the passion of Christ. In this effort to be an individual, I am completely free. This freedom comes without rules or boundaries, it also comes without a safety net. Too many people try to get through life without getting noticed, swimming in the shallows and playing in the shadows, hoping to get to the grave without causing a disturbance or being noticed. Christian existentialism challenges us to be our fullest and freest selves, dive into the depths of life, to climb upon the heights of life. In the words of Paul in Ephesians, to comprehend the breadth and length and height and depth of life, to know what surpasses knowledge, that we may be filled with the fullness of God.

We are a meaning seeking animals. We want the world to make sense, we want there to be order and reason. We look up onto the stars in all their vast randomness, and we imagine there to be constellations. Stars that are not in order, we place in order. In the language of Existentialism we encounter a world that is absurd. It is without structure and we want there to be structure, but there is no structure. That is part of our freedom. We react to this absurdity of freedom with anxiety. The exhilaration of our freedom and the dread of this chaos combine to make us anxious. Along with this chronic anxiety, we feel a sense of alienation. Because we are each unique individuals, there is a sense in which we are each alone in the universe. I am the only me. In the words of Sartre, our existence precedes our essence. We are born without meaning or purpose, and we spend our lives developing our meaning and purpose. From birth to death, we create ourselves, we finish our creation. In the words of Nietzsche we must each become an Overman. We must overcome the absurdity of our existence, our anxiety, our alienation. We must overcome our desire to become one of the many rather than one of the few, to blend in rather than stand out, to find my own way rather than follow the way of others.

For the Christian Existentialist, the death of God means there are no absolutes, no dogmas, no inherent or essential meaning. Again, we must each find our own way. It is up to us to choose, even to create the meaning and purpose of our individual lives. I am reminded of what Jesus says to his disciples in John 14:6, which I translate, "I am the true and living way." Jesus is that authentic self, that true individual, who shows us what it means to be an authentic self and a true individual. We can fully and freely become ourselves, even as he fully and freely became himself.

Christian Existentialism invites us not to discover who we are, but to create who we are. We are invited to join with God in the great cosmic dance of our own creation. To be all that we fully and freely can be. To live fully and completely in the present moment, so much so that each moment can be a moment of eternity. For the Christian existentialist, Jesus shows us how, the way it can be done. On the cross Jesus says, "It is finished." In the book of Revelation the enthroned Christ says, "It is finished." The Greek word means it is finished, accomplished, completed, made whole, fulfilled. He has finished his own self creation, and shown us that true and living way by which we may do the same. The Christian Existentialist says yes to the call and challenge of Christ. We will participate in that new creation which we may yet become. Jesus is described as embodying God's yes to us, we offer our human yes to this divine yes, accepting and affirming this call to creation and to finishing our own self creation.

WHAT NEXT?

If you have enjoyed this small volume so much that you would like to keep reading about existentialism, here are some suggestions. For Kierkegaard, read either *Purity of Heart*, which is directly Christian and a response to the beatitude of the title, or *Either-Or*, his original masterpiece. For Nietzche, *Thus Spoke Zarathustra* may be his most popular work, though *Beyond Good and Evil* would also be an excellent choice. For Heidegger, the only choice is his classic *Being and Time*. For Sartre, his *Being and Nothingness* is his response to Heidegger; his essay *Existentialism is a Humanism* is also quite accessible. For Camus, his *The Stranger*, for which he received the Nobel Prize in literature. For de Beauvoir, certainly *The Second Sex*. For Tillich, from his shorter works I recommend *The Courage to Be* as a good beginning point. From the novelists I recommend Dostoyevsky's *Crime and Punishment* or Kafka's *The Trial*. Or, if you have really enjoyed this present volume, you might just read it again!

THE VELVETEEN EXISTENTIALIST

Velveteen Rabbit by Margery Williams is a children's book with much to say to adults. I suggest you borrow a child to read it to and see what you might learn. This is a passage on being real.

> "What is real?" asked the rabbit one day. "Does it mean having things that the buzz inside you and a stick out handle?"
> "Real isn't how you are made," said the skin horse. "It's a thing that happens to you. When a child loves you for a long, long time, not just to play with, but really loves you, then you become real."
> "Does it hurt?"

"Sometimes." For he was always truthful. "When you are real you don't mind being hurt."

"Does it happen all at once, like being wound up, or bit by bit?"

"It doesn't happen all at once. You become. It takes a long time. That's why it doesn't often happen to people who break easily, or who have a sharp edges, or who have to be carefully kept. Generally, by the time you are real, most of your hair has been loved off, and your eyes and drop out and you get loose in the joints and very shabby. But these things that don't matter at all, because once you are real you can't be ugly, except to people who don't understand."

"I suppose you are real?" And then he wished he had not said it, for he thought the skin horse might be sensitive. But the skin horse only smiled.

"The boy's uncle made me real. That was a great many years ago; but once your real you can't become un-real again. It lasts for always."

The rabbit sighed he thought it would be a long time before this magic called real happened to him. He longed to become real, to know what it felt like; and yet the idea of going shabby and losing his eyes and whiskers was rather sad. He wished that he could become it without these uncomfortable things happening to him.

Existentialism is the lifelong process of becoming real. Christian existentialism is understanding that love is what makes us become real.

TOPICAL LINE DRIVES
Straight to the Point in under 44 Pages

All Topical Line Drives volumes are priced at $4.99 print and 99¢ in all ebook formats.

Available

Forthcoming

(The titles of planned volumes may change before release.)

Generous Quantity Discounts Available
Dealer Inquiries Welcome
Energion Publications — P.O. Box 841
Gonzalez, FL 32560
Website: http://energionpubs.com
Phone: (850) 525-3916

THE JESUS MANIFESTO

A PARTICIPATORY STUDY GUIDE TO

THE SERMON ON THE MOUNT

DAVID MOFFETT-MOORE

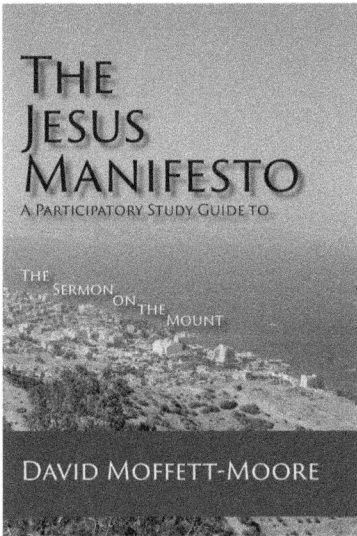

David crawled into my soul and put on paper the truth
I claim as my faith.

– **Rev. Shauna Hyde,**
Author of *Vicar of Tent Town* and
Fifty Shades of Grace

If our prayers can mature, and we can be more aware of the presence of God in every place and every moment. The purpose of this book is to help you become more aware.

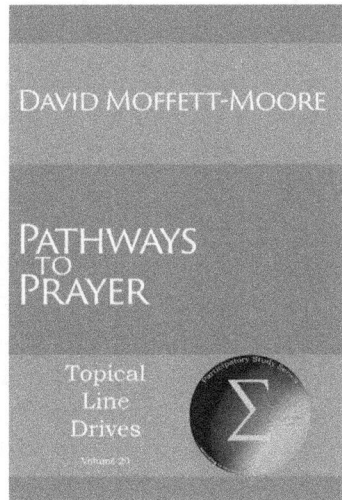

DAVID MOFFETT-MOORE

PATHWAYS TO PRAYER

Topical
Line
Drives

Σ

Volume 20

More from Energion Publications

Personal Study

Holy Smoke! Unholy Fire	Bob McKibben	$14.99
The Jesus Paradigm	David Alan Black	$17.99
When People Speak for God	Henry Neufeld	$17.99
The Sacred Journey	Chris Surber	$11.99

Christian Living

Faith in the Public Square	Robert D. Cornwall	$16.99
Grief: Finding the Candle of Light	Jody Neufeld	$8.99
Crossing the Street	Robert LaRochelle	$16.99
Life in the Spirit	J. Hamilton Weston	$12.99

Bible Study

Learning and Living Scripture	Lentz/Neufeld	$12.99
Inspiration: Hard Questions, Honest Answers	Alden Thompson	$29.99
Colossians & Philemon	Allan R. Bevere	$12.99
Ephesians: A Participatory Study Guide	Robert D. Cornwall	$9.99

Theology

Christian Archy	David Alan Black	$9.99
The Politics of Witness	Allan R. Bevere	$9.99
Ultimate Allegiance	Robert D. Cornwall	$9.99
From Here to Eternity	Bruce Epperly	$5.99
The Journey to the Undiscovered Country	William Powell Tuck	$9.99
Eschatology: A Participatory Study Guide	Edward W. H. Vick	$9.99
The Adventist's Dilemma	Edward W. H. Vick	$14.99

Ministry

Clergy Table Talk	Kent Ira Groff	$9.99
Thrive	Ruth Fletcher	$14.99
Out of the Office: A Theology of Ministry	Bob Cornwall	$9.99

Generous Quantity Discounts Available
Dealer Inquiries Welcome
Energion Publications — P.O. Box 841
Gonzalez, FL_ 32560
Website: http://energionpubs.com
Phone: (850) 525-3916

www.ingramcontent.com/pod-product-compliance
Lightning Source LLC
Chambersburg PA
CBHW021121020426
42331CB00004B/573